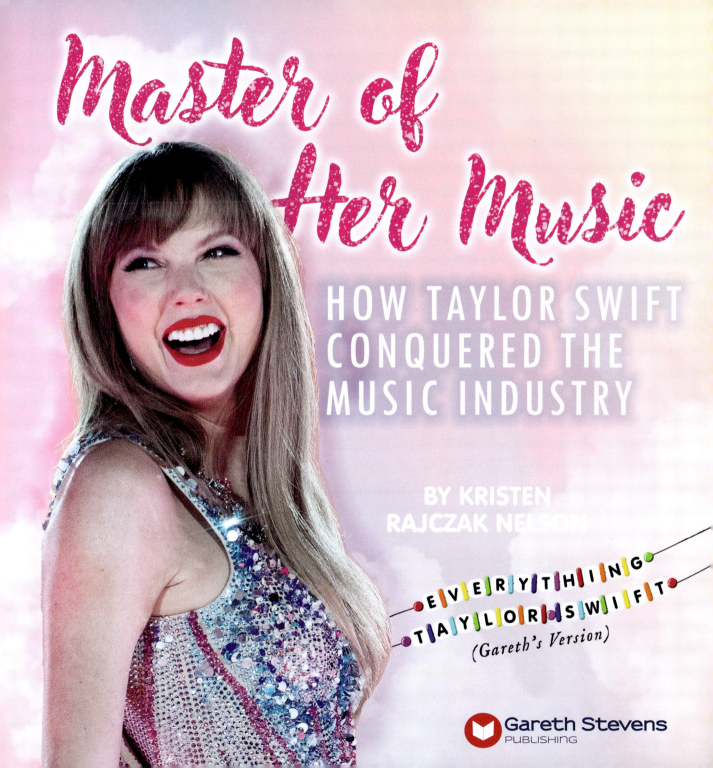

Please visit our website, www.garethstevens.com. For a free color catalog of all our high-quality books, call toll free 1-800-542-2595 or fax 1-877-542-2596.

Library of Congress Cataloging-in-Publication Data

Names: Rajczak Nelson, Kristen, author.
Title: Master of her music : how Taylor Swift conquered the music industry / Kristen Rajczak Nelson.
Description: Buffalo, New York : Gareth Stevens Publishing, 2025. | Series: Everything Taylor Swift (Gareth's version) | Includes index.
Identifiers: LCCN 2024031877 | ISBN 9781482469363 (library binding) | ISBN 9781482469356 (paperback) | ISBN 9781482469370 (ebook)
Subjects: LCSH: Swift, Taylor, 1989–Juvenile literature. | Singers–United States–Biography–Juvenile literature. | Women singers–United States–Biography–Juvenile literature.
Classification: LCC ML3930.S989 R34 2025 | DDC 782.42164092 [B]–dc23/eng/20240719
LC record available at https://lccn.loc.gov/2024031877

Published in 2025 by
Gareth Stevens Publishing
2544 Clinton Street
Buffalo, NY 14224

Copyright © 2025 Gareth Stevens Publishing

Designer: Tanya Dellaccio Keeney
Editor: Kristen Rajczak Nelson

Photo credits: Cover (friendship bracelet) Yuliqwiart/Shutterstock.com; cover (background) Haley Elizabeth/Shutterstock.com; cover (Taylor Swift) MediaPunch Inc/Alamy Images; p. 5 Courtesy of Paolo Villanueva/Flickr.com; p. 7 Aflo Co. Ltd./Alamy Images; pp. 9, 13 Everett Collection/Shutterstock.com; p. 9 (top left) Catrina Haze/Shutterstock.com; p. 11 Featureflash Photo Agency/Shutterstock.com; p. 15 https://upload.wikimedia.org/wikipedia/commons/c/ca/Taylor_Swift_RED_Tour_%288642419792%29.jpg; p. 17 a katz/Shutterstock.com; p. 19 PA Images/Alamy Images; p. 21 Tinseltown/Shutterstock.com; p. 23 Brian Friedman/Shutterstock.com; p. 25 (background) RidhamSupriyanto/Shutterstock.com; p. 26 Steve Travelguide/Shutterstock.com; p. 27 ChristinaAiko Photography/Shutterstock.com; p. 29 (notebook, pencil, paintbrush, paints) Anna Bova/Shutterstock.com; p. 29 (scissors, crayon) JuulDu/Shutterstock.com.

All rights reserved. No part of this book may be reproduced in any form without permission in writing from the publisher, except by a reviewer.

Printed in the United States of America

CPSIA compliance information: Batch #CWGS25: For further information contact Gareth Stevens at 1-800-542-2595.

Contents

THE BUSINESS OF MUSIC 4
EARLY START 6
THE FIRST DEALS. 8
COUNTRY STAR. .10
POP TO THE TOP! 14
STOP STREAMING 16
THE MASTERS 18
RIGHTS TO RERECORD 22
TAYLOR'S VERSION 24
HARDEST WORKER IN THE BUSINESS . . .28
ACTIVITY: FIND YOUR VOICE! 29
GLOSSARY 30
FOR MORE INFORMATION 31
INDEX. 32

BOLDFACE WORDS APPEAR IN THE GLOSSARY.

The Business of Music

There's no question Taylor Swift has had an effect on the music business. She successfully crossed over from country music to pop to become the biggest artist in the world. She has spoken out in favor of music artists' rights. And she has done it all while writing her own songs—hundreds of them!

Taylor is a businesswoman who makes decisions about how her music is heard. Her actions have helped shape the music **industry** of today and tomorrow!

Taylor's biggest fans are called Swifties. Taylor liked the name so much she trademarked it. That means only she can use the word in certain ways.

Taylor was just a teen when she started having to learn the business behind making music.

Early Start

Taylor started trying to get a record deal at age 11. Her mom took her to Nashville, Tennessee, to give recordings of Taylor singing to record companies. She didn't get a deal then, but Taylor kept working. She decided to write songs and learn to play the guitar. Not long after, Taylor started spending hours a day playing a 12-string guitar.

When Taylor was around 13, her family moved outside of Nashville. Taylor was chasing her musical dream!

IN TAYLOR'S WORDS

"I was from a small town, and nobody really expects you to leave, especially before you [finish high school] ... I wouldn't change a thing about growing up and not exactly fitting in. If I had been popular, I probably wouldn't have wanted to leave." (*Entertainment Weekly*, February 5, 2008)

Taylor's mom told *Entertainment Weekly* in 2008: "Don't ever say 'never' or 'can't do' to Taylor." Taylor will find a way to do it!

ANDREA SWIFT

KNOW IT ALL

Taylor was born in Pennsylvania. She lived with her mom, Andrea; her dad, Scott; and her younger brother, Austin.

The First Deals

Around the time the Swifts moved to the Nashville area, Taylor signed a songwriting deal. She went to a different company a year later. She wanted to make sure that when she made her first album, it would be her songs, not those written by someone else.

A music executive, or businessman, named Scott Borchetta saw Taylor sing in November 2004. He would later give her a record deal with his new label, Big Machine Records. Taylor put out her first album, *Taylor Swift*, in 2006.

Taylor has writing **credits** on every song on *Taylor Swift*.

Taylor Swift
BY THE NUMBERS

16 — Taylor's age when *Taylor Swift* came out

40,000 — how many albums *Taylor Swift* sold in its first week

19 — *Taylor Swift*'s first week position on the *Billboard 200* chart

11 — number of songs on *Taylor Swift*

June 19, 2006 — date Taylor's first single "Tim McGraw" came out

3 — the number of *Taylor Swift* songs Taylor is the only credited writer on:
"Should've Said No"
"The Outside"
"Our Song"

Country Star

Taylor reached young country music fans in a way that was ahead of its time. She used the early **social networking** website MySpace! Before her first album came out, Taylor had songs from it on her MySpace page to see what fans liked.

Some country stations didn't want to play Taylor's first single, "Tim McGraw." Taylor connected with fans online, asking them to push stations to play the song more often. It worked! "Tim McGraw" stayed on the Billboard Hot 100 chart for 20 weeks!

At first, "Our Song" wasn't on *Taylor Swift*. Fans on MySpace liked it so much that it was the last song added to the album!

Taylor wrote her own posts on MySpace and spoke with fans in the comments herself. This was—and still is—unusual for music artists who often hire someone to do that for them.

After *Taylor Swift* came out, Taylor went on tour. In 2006 and 2007, she opened for established country artists including Rascal Flatts, Faith Hill, Tim McGraw, and Kenny Chesney, among others. She won a Country Music **Award** (CMA) for best new artist that year too!

Taylor's next album, *Fearless*, came out at number 1 on the *Billboard* 200 album chart. Both *Fearless* and her next album, *Speak Now*, were sold as country albums. But, they had more of a pop feel. Songs like "Love Story" brought in fans beyond country music.

KNOW IT ALL

In 2007, *Taylor Swift* went platinum. This means it sold 1 million copies in the United States!

At the 2009 CMAs, Taylor won entertainer of the year as well as album of the year for *Fearless*.

Pop to the Top!

The lead single from *Red* (2012), "We Are Never Ever Getting Back Together," was Taylor's first number 1 song on the *Billboard* Hot 100, a chart of the most popular songs across all kinds of music. Still, *Red* was up for Best Country Album at the Grammy Awards.

In 2014, *1989* followed *Red*. With the first single "Shake It Off," it was clear that Taylor had fully crossed over into pop music. She did it over time, gaining fans with each step outside the country music box.

KNOW IT ALL

The album *1989* is named for the year Taylor was born! Her birthday is December 13, 1989.

Taylor played 58 shows on The Red Tour in the United States and Canada alone. She played even more around the world!

Stop Streaming

When *1989* came out in 2014, Taylor did something unthinkable at the time: She didn't allow it on the popular **streaming** service Spotify. Shortly after, she pulled all her music from Spotify. Taylor believed Spotify wasn't paying music artists fairly.

In 2015, Taylor again withheld *1989* from a streaming service. This time, it was Apple Music. She wanted Apple Music to pay music artists every time their music was streamed, even if it was during a free **trial period** for users.

Taylor kept *Red* off Spotify for a time after it came out too.

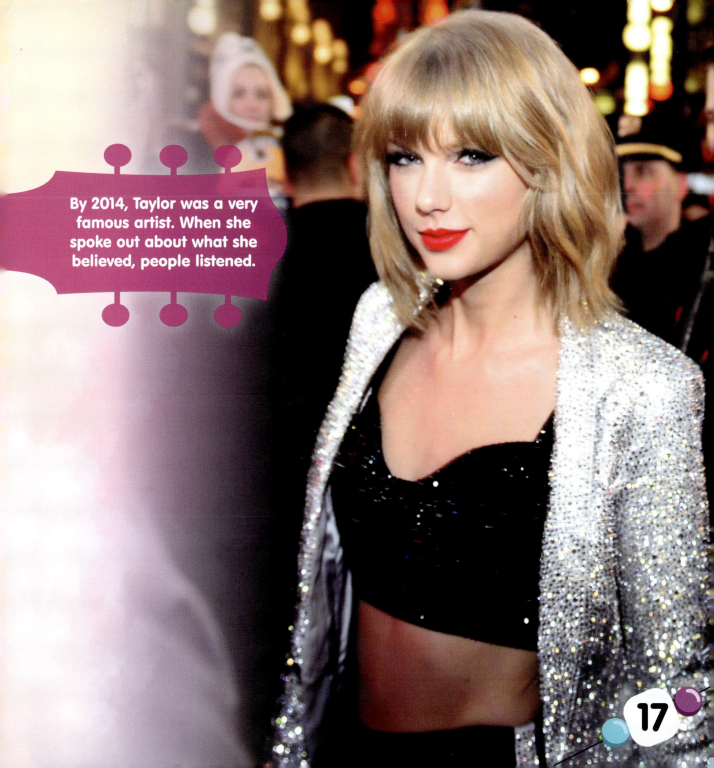

By 2014, Taylor was a very famous artist. When she spoke out about what she believed, people listened.

The Masters

Taylor made six albums with Big Machine Records, including *Reputation*, which came out in 2017. Her contract had a common part to it: The company owned the **master recordings** of all Taylor's songs. As her contract ended in 2018, she wanted to own those masters.

Then, Taylor signed a deal with a different company, Republic Records. This time, her contract said she would own all the master recordings of the music she made with Republic. When *Lover* came out in 2019, Taylor owned her music like never before!

In June 2017, Taylor allowed her music to be put back on all streaming services. She had sold 100 million songs worldwide and said she wanted to thank her fans.

In 2019, the video for Taylor's song "You Need to Calm Down" from *Lover* won video of the year at the MTV Video Music Awards (VMAs).

In 2019, Scooter Braun bought Big Machine Records. He now owned the master recordings for the albums Taylor made with Big Machine. Because of this, Big Machine tried to stop Taylor from performing older songs at the 2019 American Music Awards or using them in her **documentary** *Miss Americana*. Taylor asked fans to voice their anger—and they did! Taylor was allowed to use her music for both.

Then, Scooter sold Taylor's master recordings again. He made hundreds of millions of dollars on the deal! Taylor was angry. She felt she didn't get enough of a chance to buy her own masters.

Taylor is one of the first artists to openly talk about wanting to own master recordings. What happened to her will likely have an effect on future contracts in the music business.

Rights to Rerecord

Taylor still had some ownership of her music. She was a credited writer on every song on every album she had put out. This gave her something called publishing rights. Publishing rights include the lyrics and melody, or words and music, to a song.

Because she had publishing rights to her songs, Taylor was able to rerecord her songs after a certain period of time. By doing this, she would then own master recordings of all her music!

IN TAYLOR'S WORDS

"I think that artists deserve to own their work. I feel very **passionate** about that."
(*Good Morning America*, August 2019)

One reason Taylor may have wanted to own masters of her work is that she can decide whether it is used in TV and movies—and get paid for its use!

Taylor's Version

Taylor began rerecording her albums. Each album was released with the same name with "Taylor's **Version**" after it. *Fearless (Taylor's Version)* came out in April 2021. *Red (Taylor's Version)* quickly followed in November.

Both albums had the same songs in the same order. But Taylor included additional tracks that didn't make the original albums. This was one way Taylor attracted, or drew in, fans to buy new versions of old albums. A fan favorite was the 10-minute version of the song "All Too Well" found on *Red (Taylor's Version)*.

IN TAYLOR'S WORDS

"When I created [these songs], I didn't know what they would grow up to be. Going back in and knowing that it meant something to people is actually a really beautiful way to celebrate what the fans have done for my music."
(*Billboard*, December 11, 2019)

Taylor's Albums

2006 — Taylor Swift
2008 — FEARLESS
2010 — Speak Now
2012 — RED
2014 — 1989
2017 — reputation
2019 — Lover
2020 — folklore and evermore
2021 — FEARLESS (Taylor's Version) and RED (Taylor's Version)
2022 — Midnights
2023 — Speak Now (Taylor's Version) and 1989 (Taylor's Version)
2024 — THE TORTURED POETS DEPARTMENT and THE TORTURED POETS DEPARTMENT: THE ANTHOLOGY

As each new version of an older album came out, Taylor asked fans to support that album instead of the original. Fans updated playlists on streaming services and bought Taylor's Version albums in huge numbers.

Limited-edition **merchandise** came out with each Taylor's Version release. Fans bought it all, including **vinyl** records and CDs with different covers. The fact that Taylor could sell **physical** copies of her albums was special. Some fans had likely bought the original albums too—and now owned a copy of the original and the Taylor's Version!

TOP-SELLING ALBUM OF 2023

SOLD 1.65 MILLION COPIES IN THE FIRST WEEK

OUTSOLD *1989* IN THE FIRST WEEK BY ABOUT 360,000 COPIES

11.6 MILLION PEOPLE AROUND THE WORLD STREAMED "STYLE (TAYLOR'S VERSION)" ON SPOTIFY THE DAY IT CAME OUT

1989 (Taylor's Version) was a huge hit!

BROKE HER OWN RECORD OF MOST-STREAMED ARTIST IN A SINGLE DAY WITH *1989 (TAYLOR'S VERSION)* RELEASE

Hardest Worker in the Business

Taylor did more than put out Taylor's Versions of *Speak Now*, *Fearless*, *Red*, and *1989* between 2021 and 2023. She also put out two new albums in 2020, and *Midnights* in 2022. She released *The Tortured Poets Department* in 2024. Starting in 2023, she traveled the world on The Eras Tour.

This makes it clear: Taylor Swift has made her name in the music industry through hard work! She stands up for herself. And she connects with her fans through music that is truly hers.

The Eras Tour is the highest-grossing—or most money-making—concert tour of all time!

Activity: Find Your Voice!

Taylor speaks up when she believes something is unfair. What do you believe in? What do you think isn't right? Use this activity to help you stand up for what you believe in!

IDEA #1
MAKE A POSTER

Do you support a new town recycling program? Do you want to encourage people to give money to the local animal shelter? Write a catchy phrase in support of your belief. Then, spread the word by making a colorful poster with the phrase and putting it in your front yard!

IDEA #2
START A CLUB

Do you wish your school or community had painting classes? Do you think cyberbullying is a big problem in your class? Gather a group of friends to start a club! Write a letter inviting others to join and ask a teacher to help you pass it out at school.

IDEA #3
WRITE A LETTER

Don't like something your local government or congressperson has done? Write them a letter telling them why! Better yet, gather friends who feel the same way and write letters together!

Glossary

award: A prize given for doing something.

credit: Recognition of someone by name of their work on something.

documentary: A movie or TV show presenting information about an issue or person.

industry: The businesses that offer one kind of service or product.

master recording: The official, original recording of a song. It is sometimes just called a master.

merchandise: Goods sold by an artist such as T-shirts and posters.

passionate: Showing great feeling.

physical: Having to do with something that can be held in your hands.

social networking: Having to do with websites and apps that allow people to communicate with one another through posts, videos, and comments.

stream: To transfer data in a continuous way, meant to be watched or listened to immediately.

trial period: A time when a user tries out a service, often without paying for it.

version: A form of something that is different from others.

vinyl: A kind of plastic used to make records.

For More Information

Books

Burk, Rachelle. *The Story of Taylor Swift: An Inspiring Biography for Young Readers*. Naperville, IL: Callisto Publishing, 2024.

Gottlieb, Beth. *Taylor Swift*. Buffalo, NY: Enslow Publishing, 2024.

Websites

Taylor Swift
www.taylorswift.com/
Keep up with Taylor on her official website.

Taylor Swift: Artist
www.grammy.com/artists/taylor-swift/15450
Find out more about the Grammy Awards Taylor has been nominated for and won.

Publisher's note to educators and parents: Our editors have carefully reviewed these websites to ensure that they are suitable for students. Many websites change frequently, however, and we cannot guarantee that a site's future contents will continue to meet our high standards of quality and educational value. Be advised that students should be closely supervised whenever they access the internet.

Index

Apple Music, 16

Big Machine Records, 8, 18, 20

birthday, 14

Braun, Scooter, 20

Fearless, 12, 13, 24, 25, 28

guitar, 6

Lover, 18, 19, 25

"Love Story," 12

Miss Americana, 20

mom, 6, 7

MySpace, 10, 11

Nashville, Tennessee, 6

1989, 14, 16, 25, 27

publishing rights, 22

Red, 14, 16, 25, 28

Republic Records, 18

Reputation, 18, 25

Speak Now, 12, 25, 28

Spotify, 16, 27

Taylor Swift, 8, 9, 10, 12, 25

Tortured Poets Department, The, 25, 28

tours, 12, 15, 28